A CHILD'S GRACE

AUTHOR & ILLUSTRATOR ELLEN BUTTACAVOLI

A Child's Grace from Heaven

v3.0

This is a work of fiction. The events and characters described herein are imaginary and are not intended to refer to specific places or living persons. The opinions expressed in this manuscript are solely the opinions of the author and do not represent the opinions or thoughts of the publisher. The author has represented and warranted full ownership and/or legal right to publish all the materials in this book.

Outskirts Press, Inc.
http://www.outskirtspress.com

ISBN: 978-1-9772-3418-6

PRINTED IN THE UNITED STATES OF AMERICA

outskirts press

This Book Belongs to:

____

Now I lay me down to sleep
I pray the Lord my soul to keep

When I awake all fresh and new
Please guide me Lord in all I do.

Please bless my parents while they work
my Mom's a Nurse, my Dad's a Bank clerk

Please bless my Grandma and Grandpa who's eighty
my Brother and Sister who's just a small baby.

2 + 2 = 4
4 + 3 = 7
CAT

Please help me Lord while I'm in school
To add, subtract and follow the rules
It's fun to learn new things and read
My teacher will help me to succeed

When I get home, I want to play
but Mom say's I have chores today.

When I am done its time for fun
I'll ride my bike and enjoy the sun.

Today is Sunday,
we all go to Church
I love it there; we sing
and we search

for understanding, faith and love
We praise our sweet Jesus who is so beloved.

We should say grace before we eat
and bless the farmers who grow wheat.

We thank you Lord for our good food
Our hearts are full of gratitude.

Please bless the trees and birds that chirp,
The mountains and oceans, excuse me, I burped!

And once again,
it"s time for bed.
I'll fluff my pillow
and rest my head

I always pray before I sleep
or else I will be counting sheep

Now I lay me down to sleep
I pray the Lord my soul to keep

If I get scared and want to cry
I'll sing this little Lullaby

A Child's Prayer

by Natalya A. Bencivenga

Hail Mary full of grace
Bless my friends of every race

Tall and short or young and old
From way down south to where it's cold

Please Bless our world from any harm
My prayers to you will keep me calm

And as I close my sleepy eyes,
I know your always by my side.

Hail Mary Prayer

Hail Mary full of grace

the Lord is with thee

Blessed art thou among women

And blessed is the fruit

Of thy womb Jesus.

Holy Mary Mother of God,

Pray for us sinners

Now and at the hour

of our death

Amen

I'll try to learn this blessed prayer

I know your with me everywhere.

The Lord's Prayer

Our Father, who art in heaven,

Hallowed be thy name.

Thy Kingdom come,

Thy will be done,

On earth as it is in heaven.

Give us this day our daily bread.

And forgive us our trespasses,

as we forgive those

Who trespass against us.

And lead us not into temptation,

But deliver us from evil

Amen

A Child's Prayer verses

words by Ellen Buttacavoli

music by Natalya A. Bencivenga

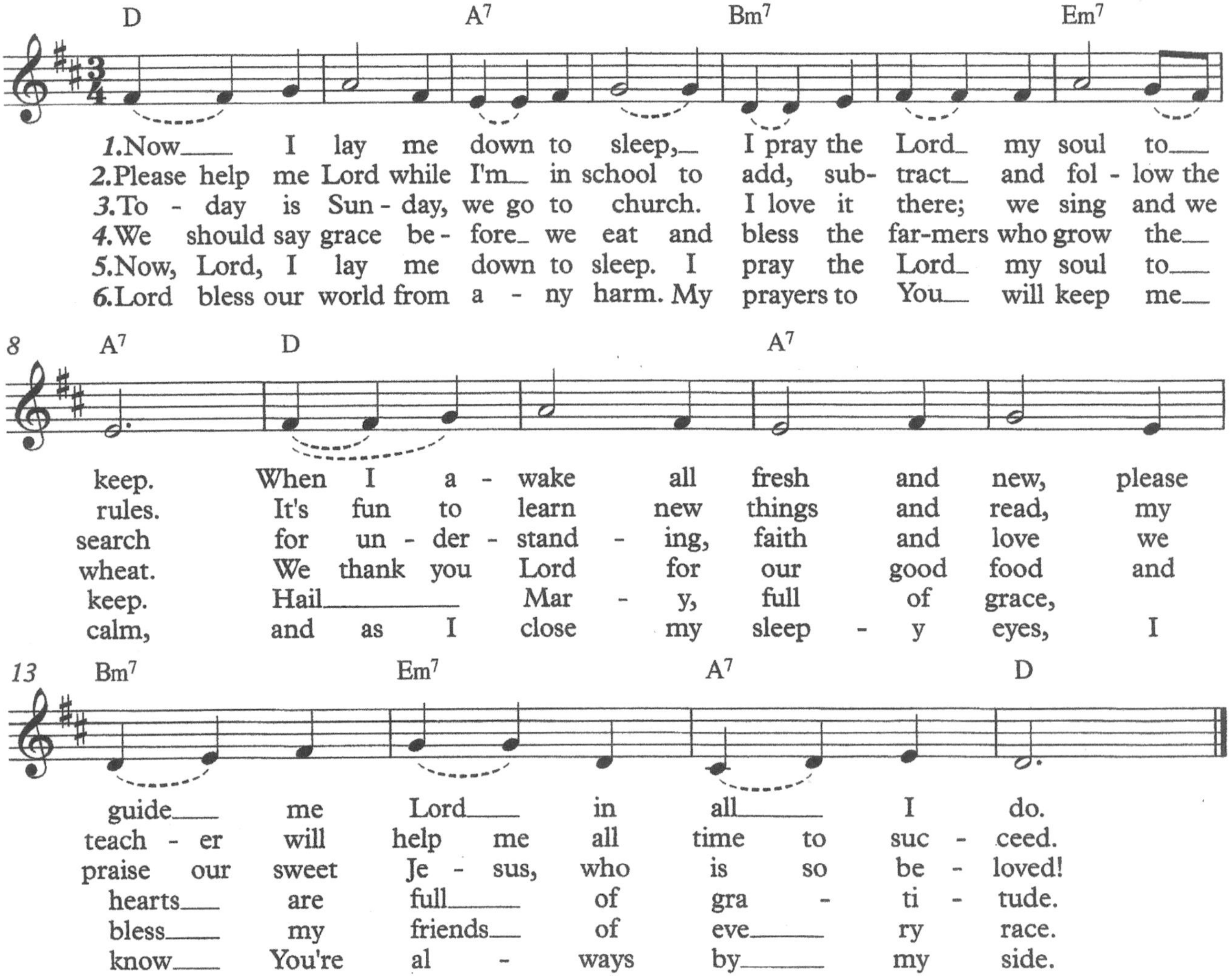

LULLABY song by Natalya
can be found on YOU TUBE
And you can order more books
at AMAZON.com under A Childs Grace by Ellen Buttacavoli

CPSIA information can be obtained
at www.ICGtesting.com
Printed in the USA
BVHW020410230321
603053BV00001B/1

* 9 7 8 1 9 7 7 2 3 4 1 8 6 *